AND THEN YOU KNOW

KWAME ALEXANDER

Published by Word of Mouth Books
PO Box 21
Alexandria, VA 22313

Some of these poems have appeared in *Native Magazine, 100 Greatest African American Poems, Beltway Poetry Quarterly, Warpland, Gargoyle, Grandfathers: Reminiscences, Poems, Recipes, and Photos of the Keepers of Our Traditions, The NYSEC Journal, Wordhouse, Tuesdays, Urban Code, Fledgling Rag,* and on *Facebook.*

FIRST PAPERBACK EDITION
ISBN: 978-1479120475

Jacket Photos by Pilar Vergara
10 9 8 7 6 5 4 3 2 1
Printed in the U.S.A.

for Steph

ACKNOWLEDGMENTS

I am so very grateful for the Book-in-a-Day International Fellows who have become dear friends and the best writing community one could ever hope to be a part of: Deanna, Marj, Randy, Chris, Dana, Kim, Tinesha, Nana, and Marjie, Van. *Grazie and Obrigado to you all!*

CONTENTS

If I Were A Poet In Love…

A Letter From a Man to His Woman 12
Good night 13
If You Were A Couplet, I'd Rhyme You 15
Kupenda 17
Chesapeake 18
Picturing You 19
Southern Love Song 20
Kupenda 22
Spellbound 23
April 24
Kupenda 25
Tanka 26
Corepoem 27
Haiku 28
Sublunary 29
Kupenda 30
In My Closet, On The Top Shelf, Is A Silver Box 31
Renga 33
Awkward Poems 34
Kupenda 36
Letter to AfroDite 37
Revolutionary Love Poem 40
'S Incredible 43
Real World 45

Come Samayah, Dance With Me…

Ten Reasons Why Fathers Cry at Night 48
Good Morning Sunshine 49
My Father's Eulogy 50
Haiku for My Mother 50

Separate but Equal 52
Nandi 53
Daughterlove 54
Letter to My Brother 55
The Remembering 58
Acts of Love 61
A Letter to My Daughter 63

If You Were A Song, I'd Call You Jazz…

A Nikki Poem 70
Tanka 71
After reading E. Ethelbert Miller 72
Kupenda 73
After Listening to Beware the Short Hair Girl 74
Drive 75
For Bessie Coleman 77
A Borrowed Poem 78
For Nikki Giovanni 79
A Poem Commemorating the Inauguration of Barack Obama 80
Haiku 82

At Least I'll Have Poetry…

Dancing Naked on the Floor 84
Our Women 86
When 88
Memo to Company President 89
Soul on Fire 90
Renga 93
Im(us) Be Crazy 94
Betty 96
Daddy 98
How We Love 99
Just Us 101
Life 102

Heroes, Gods, and Me 103
On Being Asked By A Middle School Student... 104
Ebony Images 105
Where Do We Go From Here? 106
Buck and Wing/The Flow 107

I Find Poems in the Strangest Places. Between your...

Haiku 112
Kupenda 113
A Thought 114
Kupenda 115
Why I Like The Post Office 116
Haiku 117
Haiku 117
Kupenda 118
You Make Me Want To 119
Negril 120
Haiku 121
Haiku 121
Kupenda 122
Haiku 123

In 1994 I produced a play based on the Jess B. Semple stories of Langston Hughes. Semple pretty much summed it up when he said, "The first time I was in love, I was in love stone-dead-bad, because I had it, and it had me, and it was the most!" That year, I decided I was going to be a poet and a playwright. So, naturally, I embraced public transportation. It would be years before I sold enough poetry books to buy a used car. I guess I got lucky, because I began courting a woman who lived only a few miles from me. So, every evening I'd walk to her house, downhill to visit with her (and every night she'd send me back home. Walking. Uphill). I was in love. Bad. For almost a year, I'd fax her poems and notes and thoughts. Every morning. This became our ritual. I guess my legs became a little tired from all the back (i was cool with the forth) because one day, as we were walking from seven eleven, I casually mentioned that I needed some time. Some space. To figure out what i wanted. She said 'okay,' like I'd just asked her if I could borrow some sugar. Then she casually continued sipping her slurpee. Four years later I married her. And I'd do it again. One million times, if i could (recylcing the ring, of course); 'because I had it, and it had me, and it was the most!'

A LETTER FROM A MAN TO HIS WOMAN

I have been underwater
my entire life
You pull me up,
introduce me
to new breath,
strange and familiar
This is where I want to be
Between the river
inside your arms
carefully inhaling
tomorrow

(2008)

GOOD NIGHT

According to Google
there are five phases of sleep.
Somewhere between two

and three I shift to my right side
If you are woken up during this stage,
you may feel groggy and disoriented

I move my hand from
my forehead, ready for the slow
delta waves of deep sleep

If phase three is too short, sleep
will not feel satisfying.
Are you awake, she asks?

I am on the edge of falling
Is someone calling my name?
Should I answer?

My wife is aware
that I am a light sleeper
she knows that the hint

of a glimmer or mild cacophony
will send me back to phase one:
The eyes are closed, but if aroused…

Wait,
Someone is calling my name
Are you awake?

I see her now. Leaning

against the cherry headboard. Staring
at me. Concerned, confounded

curious. I wonder, have I forgotten
something significant. Birthday, anniversary,
dishes.

Why don't you write me
Love poems anymore?
She asks. At 3 am.

Should I answer?
I open the other eye
seeing her full on

I sit up, inch a little
closer to her naked land
You are still my ocean,

My dear. Your hips my
soft raft. Those two lips the oars
I steer. You are the poem

If you were a couplet
I'd rhyme you
Okay, she smiles

Just don't haiku me
Take yr time
I want an Epic

Anything else, my dear?
Well, since you're up
Can you take care of the dishes?

(2009)

IF YOU WERE A COUPLET,
I'D RHYME YOU

If you were a ladder
I'd climb you

Way up to the top
and I'd find you

If you were a doorway
I'd enter you

If you were unhinged
I'd center you

If you were a secret
I'd uncover you

Then seek out your treasure
rediscover you

If you were in front
I'd behind you

Pull out some espresso
and grind you

Let's say you're a Bossa
I'd hum you

Play you my guitar
and strum you

If you weren't my wife
I'd wed you

Then pull out a quilt
and I'd bed you

But, since you're my woman
I'll just love you

And kiss that sweet halo
above you

(2009)

KUPENDA 22

I've never been a slave
Yet, I know I am whipped
I've never escaped underground
Yet, the night knows my journey
I've never been to Canada
Yet, I've crossed your border
If I were a poet in love
I'd say that
with you
I have found that new place
where romance
is just a beginning
and freedom
is our end.

(1997)

CHESAPEAKE, VIRGINIA

An odd pair
A country boy
An ugly girl
A playful peck
A childhood friend
A decade later
A senior prom
An awkward question
A long wait
A final answer
A rented tux
A lobster dinner
A sparkling cider
An empty wallet
A last dance
A second kiss
A great time
A promised tomorrow
A beautiful woman
A country boy
An odd pair
A Chesapeake memory

(2000)

PICTURING YOU

I am not a painter
Browns and blues
We get along
But we
are not close
I am no
Van Gogh
But give me
Plain paper
A dull pencil
Some scotch
And I will
Hijack your curves
Take your soul
Hostage
Paint a portrait
So colorful and delicate
You just may have to
Cut off my ear

(2003)

SOUTHERN LOVE SONG

I know my honey
cares for me
see, i asked her for a dollar
and she gave me three

Now i've dated a lot of girls in my life
but this here woman's gon' be my wife

I know my sugar's
love is true
see, i told my momma
and she told hers too

Now i've dated a lot of girls in my life
but this here woman's gon' be my wife

I know my baby's
heart is mine
see, she tells me all the time
I'm fine

Now i've dated a lot of girls in my life
but this here woman's gon' be my wife

My baby's been askin'
how's i feel
wants to know
is my feelings real

So i proceeds to kiss her
on her lips
politely place my hands
on her hips

Whisper these words
in her ear
and hope she don't get too excited
to hear

That i've dated a lot of girls in my life
But you, one day, gon' be my wife

(1994)

KUPENDA 85

if only words could marry
just maybe mine might
put a ring on your verse
and make beautiful couplets
that dance naturally
from our sweet rhythm

(2008)

SPELLBOUND

without u
i am lost

as in: isolated
unfinished   broken off

shipwrecked on the shore of solitude
ankle deep in possibility

i have read the dictionary
twice

and still there r no words
to fill my blank spaces

to punctuate the way i feel
when your smile dances

across the stucco walls
of my memory

perhaps
i will open a thesaurus now

and find a little piece of hope
or something similar

(2004)

APRIL

inside
the Spring r soft

poems of would be
lovers etched

in desire
on lonely sheets

of the Sun's journal.
u r my book

and with
delight

i write on...
and on

(1996)

KUPENDA 36
(FOR SAMARACA)

I am not a flamethrower
nor do I drive a red truck   yet
i have this
burning desire
in the seat
of my palm
at the hearth
of my existence
to marry you
        over

            and over
perhaps, one million times
(recycling the ring, of course)
        the very thought
of saying "I do"
over
and over
wd set my soul
on fire
and I could
breathe
again…

(1999)

TANKA

sleeping alone is
a nightmarish journey
barefoot on Everest
mosquitoes in paradise
Marcus Garvey without ship

(2004)

COREPOEM

the grasp of the earth
and the softness of the wind
were most definitely something
but not until i witnessed
the journey of
one thousand waves
through the swelling waters
of your ocean
did i understand
the meaning of
gravity

(1989)

HAIKU

the things that matter
you you you you you you   then
everything else

(2008)

SUBLUNARY

it is not that we love
                  suddenly
like two track stars
coming from behind
                  edging
to the finish line
it is that we have loved
                  effortlessly
for one thousand seasons
                  sprinting
cross memory
                  jogging
through the night
on the heels of Isis
ours
is a long distance love
that will always be
time and space,
our hurdles
two poets
                  dancing
under
the moon

(2004)

KUPENDA 92

This is what I know
friendship is an art
and this canvas called life
can be vast and lonesome
without a full heart to trust
without a joyful noise to share
without you

(2008)

IN MY CLOSET, ON THE TOP SHELF, IS A SILVER BOX

Journal, filled
Candy bar, unwrapped
Picture, Kevin
Tulips, Kevin
Poems, Kevin
Library card, mine
Naomi Shihab's *What Have You Lost?* overdue
Saturday, late
Us, movies
Laughing, loving
Later, strolling
Me, "I want chocolate"
Kevin, "You already sweet enough, baby"
Store, closing
We, hurrying
Colliding, customer
Accident, sorry
Guy, angry
Me, craving
Kevin, Hershey
We, pay
Turn, leave
Surprise, a rose,
Pink, favorite
Me, "thanks"
Outside, "Hey!"
Guy, earlier
Kevin, ignore
Hands, holding
Walking, fast
Giant, steps
Me, turn

Guy, points
aims, fires
rips, back
Kevin, drops
candy, sidewalk
Rose, falls
Guy, runs
Blood, runs
Kevin, "You alright?"
Me, "Kevin!"
Eyes, closing
Me, "I Love You"
Kevin, "More than a Kit Kat?"
We, laugh
Sirens, scream
Heart, pierced
Love, bleeds
Hope, dies
Hands, empty
Sweetness of life, gone
What, remains
Picture, Kevin
Flower, Kevin
Candy bar, unopened
Locked, away
Inside, silver box
top shelf, in my closet

(2007)

RENGA
(AFTER DINNER CONVERSATION)

he says

you are an angel
show me your heaven, watch me
kneel down, speak in tongues

she answers

let's exchange haiku
instead make me pregnant with
yr muscular words

he frowns

woman don't resist me
clean out your basement let me
move in stay awhile

with puckered brow, she replies

is that all you know, love poems
I'm busy, there is much work

to be done around
here write me a freedom poem
one that fires up
lame democrats removes Bush
better yet, write me one that

cleans house.

(2004)

AWKWARD POEMS

Sometimes I wish we weren't friends
then i could gaze into your bold eyes
and find answers to questions i'm afraid to ask
but for now, i'll stick to quick glances
and other friendly gestures

Sometimes i wish we weren't friends
then i could hold your hands in ways
that made your palms moist from wet suggestion
but for now, i'll stick to high fives
and other friendly gestures

Sometimes i wish we weren't friends
then i could eclipse your moon baked, ruby red crescents
with my sun-starved, cherry-coated lips
but for now, i'll stick to light pecks
and other friendly gestures

Sometimes i wish we weren't friends
then i could kneel before your delicate temple
grasp you in my full arms,
as we embrace into the morning
but for now, i'll stick to daylight hugs
and other friendly gestures

What i am trying to say is
I love
glancing into your big eyes
touching your soft hands
kissing your dark cheeks
hugging your warm body
and being your friend

but one day
one day real soon
i'm gonna put away those
big
soft
dark
friendly gestures
and get close
get real close to you

but for now, i'll stick to awkward poems
and other friendly gestures

(1994)

KUPENDA 93

If only
I cd autograph

Yr voice
Paint

My signature
On yr tongue

Write each letter
Between

Yr lips
Have you sing

My name
If only

I cd autograph
Yr heart

(2008)

LETTER TO AFRODITE

I watched
yr hair transform
itself
the way my soul did
the first time I felt
yr voice
and wondered if
u and I cd ever be
as tight
as the cornrows
that crown yr
spirit

now, my eyes r liquid
a mighty sheen
and they r all over u
and they r all over u
and they r all over u
on top
wishing u wd make
that switch to some ole'
shea butter
so I can nestle deep
w/in those parts
between

perhaps one day
perhaps
one day
when water is free
and heat is complimentary
when hugging is mandatory
and love is ongoing (even when it ain't supposed to be)

when hotels don't charge for local calls
and shoes don't cost so much
when poets read books
and not just their own
when perms r permanent
and everybody's natural
when sex is safe
and sons have fathers
u know
the way things are supposed to be

perhaps one day
when time permits
and yr couch has been delivered
i will place u betwixt
my legs
and
unravel your thick past
comb through yr fine future
repair any damage
so we can lock
and grow
as one
a double helix coming
together
searching for
a truth
meant to be
and finding it
until then
I will write like it's 1969
and u r nikki giovanni
and i am h. rap brown
and we will bring our heads together

           Our poems shall be
         Married and birth beautiful
              Black baby haikus

that will nurture our vision
determine our direction
confirm our destiny
to live these braided fantasies
on paper
in love poems
like the one u read
that first time
and made me wonder
if u and i cd ever be
as tight
as the cornrows
crowning yr spirit

all of this,
and i don't even know

your last name

(1999)

REVOLUTIONARY LOVE POEM

Got up this morning
Feeling good and black
Thinking black thoughts
Did black things
Played all my black records
And minded my own black bidness
Put on my best black clothes
Walked out my black door
And…
Lord Have Mercy
White
Snow!

—Jackie Early "1,968 Winters"

I once read a love poem
At a revolutionary meeting:

you quenched my
sun-rayed thirst
the moonbeaming
her
in/two
our life

And nobody clapped.
I once read a love poem
At a revolutionary meeting:

the sun melted slowly
the day u left
and when u called
i froze

And the brothers shouted "ain't that
counterrevolutionary, talk about The Man."
I once read a love poem
At a revolutionary meeting:

on lonely nights
while 2nd floor
traffic noises loom
thru the air
i dream
of being in yr
blk ride
sometimes driving

And the sisters screamed "ain't gon'
be no cars in the revolution, talk about
The Man."

I once read a love poem
At a revolutionary meeting:

Yr movement is fluid
Like a river running deep
I am careful not to drown

And they told me to "sit down"
'cause I won't talking about
The Revolution.

The next time I read a love poem
At a revolutionary meeting
I'll make sure and tell the "revolutionaries"
That there will be no revolution
Until we learn how to respect our women
Until we learn how to treat out men
Until we learn how to love each other

I'll make sure and tell the "revolutionaries"
That fightin' "The Man" is moot
If we ain't got a plan to start
Lovin' one another
I'll make sure and tell the "revolutionaries"
That the biggest problem facing us in the 21st century is
Us

Once we love
We can create
You dig?
Then dig yourself a black hole and peep this…

They asked me to read a blacklovepoem
At a revolutionary meeting

Got up this morning
Feeling good and Black
Hugged my black wife
Kissed my black child
Ate black food
Took my daughter to a black school
And shopped at all black stores
Came back to my black house
Opened my black mind
And…
Lord Have Mercy
A Revolution!

(1996)

'S INCREDIBLE

Call me
I want to hear your soul
Surround me
The symphony of you
astounds me
Won't you play our
Secret melody
Just for you and me

Touch me
The way your full lips
Wrap around me
Makes me want to want you
Solely
Won't you play our
Secret melody
Just for you and me

Don't you know your Coltrane
Keeps me
Captivates me
so completely
When your Sarah
Sings so close to me
'S incredible

Find me
Where the blues will not
Deceive me
In a place where love is
Easy
Won't you play our

Secret melody
Just for you and me

Don't you know your Coltrane
Keeps me
Captivates me
so completely
When your Sarah
Sings so close to me
'S incredible

Note: 'S Incredible is a song, with lyrics written by Kwame Alexander, Lauri Preston, Cozetta Green, and Ken Mobley at Vinx's Songwriter's Soul Kitchen in McRae, Georgia

(2008)

REAL WORLD

she tells me they
only sell books about

social justice and
peace and that mine are mostly

about love and
relationships which they

don't promote.
i ask her if she thought

changing the world by
herself was such a good

idea and how could you ever
be free without

someone to hold
i wonder how many

revolutions started with a
kiss how many communists Neruda

made love to how free it must
feel to walk through life

at peace
alone

(2008)

For fun, we traveled. Summer road trips. Florida for Christmas. We'd go to Hunan Park East in Manhattan every year for Thanksgiving. In hindsight, these adventures were treasures for young minds, but what we really wanted to do as kids, we couldn't: Watch TV. We were allowed to watch one TV show per week, usually a weekend show. I caught Different Strokes on Friday nights. My father was a preacher, a book publisher, a historian, and an author. He wrote more than 15 books and my siblings and I were consistently "encouraged" to read each of them. My mother was a professional storyteller who taught English, and we were consistently being told about the dangers of ending a sentence with a preposition. We certainly preferred her folktales to his tomes, but we complained about it all, craving a life outside of their literary and artistic boxes. Fast forward (a few decades), and one of us is a photographer, one is in the music business, another a model, and the other a poet. I guess we showed them. Each of us has our own children now. Some of us have teenagers. They all complain. They all want to be left alone to their lives. They all have frequent flyer miles. They do get to watch more than one TV show per week though. Two. (Isn't life grand?)

TEN REASONS WHY FATHERS CRY AT NIGHT

1. Because fifteen-year-olds don't like park swings or long walks anymore unless you're in the mall

2. Because holding her hand is forbidden and kisses are lethal

3. Because school was "fine," her day was "fine," and yes, she's "fine." (So why is she weeping?)

4. Because you want to help, but you can't read minds

5. Because she is in love and that's cute, until you find his note asking her to prove it

6. Because she didn't prove it

7. Because next week she is in love again and this time it's real, she says her heart is heavy

8. Because she yearns to take long walks in the park with him

9. Because you remember the myriad woes and wonders of spring desire

10. Because with trepidation and thrill you watch your daughter who suddenly wants to swing all by herself

(2005)

GOOD MORNING SUNSHINE

Come Samayah dance with me
unclose your eyes and glance at me
unfurl those arms to France for me
Now, come Samayah dance with me

Come Samayah swing with me
won't you be kind and sing for me
it might as well be spring to me
Now, come Samayah swing with me

Come Samayah read with me
Please read some Socrates to me
But first your ABCs for me
Now, come Samayah read with me

Come Samayah play with me
Let's have a big soiree for me
And cha cha cha away with me
Now, come Samayah play with me

Come Samayah dance with me
You must let go your trance for me
Won't you please take a stance with me
And boogie woogie dance with me

(2009)

MY FATHER'S EULOGY

My Father
rests alone
at home
and questions why
his sisters
chose
another man
to pray.
The last time
his Mother died
they did
the same
but he obliged
and sat beside
another man
who said goodbye
to Granny.
Only this time
he couldn't
bear the thought
of losing
twice.
And so
at home
alone
he sat away
from flowers
open graves
saving tears
for the future's
sure unrest
endless nights

spent reciting
his Father's Eulogy
to himself.

(1998)

HAIKU
FOR BARBARA

there wd be no books
without the childhood poems the
playful way u loved

(2005)

SEPARATE BUT EQUAL

my mother
has moved
beyond this institution
of warped
western expectations
above this drama
of soap opera
divisiveness
she is happily dating
her husband once again
proving that real love
continues on
even when it ain't supposed to

(1999)

NANDI

looks twelve
although she is a busy nine
lives happily with her mother
reads a lot
questions everything
can identify a Campbell
by the neck
knows each of the Pinkneys
recites poetry in school
is certain to lock her diary
wants to be a figure-skating Publisher
collects dolls like pennies
sells cookies to her neighbors
speaks Swahili with her Granny
dances ballet and Dreamgirls
listens to Ellington
skis without fear
writes Spanish
sings Gospel
goes to Macedonia twice a week
and still finds time
to make her lunch
the night before
while asking
how my day was

(2000)

DAUGHTERLOVE

now
at the mall
on a bench
waiting
on this new woman
i watch her becoming
something is good
she is pleased
her smile
walks my way
i am poised
finally for
some sweet salutation
alas,
can i have another 20?
and
as my hand
digs denim
i can't imagine
never having
another 20 for
this wonder of mine
this woman
becoming

(2007)

LETTER TO MY BROTHER

how many times must we
casually watch
the downpour
drain the hope
and life
from our streets
before we find our minds
before we go uncrazy?
i want to tell you i have the answer
but i don't
and my arms cannot reach you
this time

we, who can still dance
we, who can still skate the sky
we, who can touch the earth
are not blameless
in this aching moment
and while this is not
a simple apology
i want to tell you that
my sorrow is grave
i want to remind you that life has not
worn out its welcome

i can hear
the shrieks and screams
lingering beneath the cool
didhedidhedidhedidhedidhe
    saysaysaysaysaysay
    nononononononononononono
    howhowhowhowhowhowhowhow
    isheisheisheisheisheishe

i want to tell her that
you will be all right
your heart strong
that this is just one more river to cross
      nonononononononononononono
      howhowhowhowhowhowhowhow
      isheisheisheisheisheishe
i want to envelope you
send you back across the pain
because this middle passage
has killed our center
and makes me wonder
if those who jumped
were the sane ones
and the rest of us, well,
need help

later, we will sit in silence
our cries gone unheard
our faith questioned
      howhowhowhowhowhowhowhow
      hewonthewonthewonthewont
but you will
because you owe that to yourself
because if you don't, we don't either
because, i want to tell you,
my arms cannot reach you
this time

you are Buddha drifting
in quicksand
yr calm as thick as heavy rain
yr freedom as sure as sliding mud
and while my fingers are crossed
i want to tell you
that this storm will not last

that the sun will escape
but it won't
and my arms cannot reach you
this time

(2005)

THE REMEMBERING

One day next winter
after you've been gone
twenty seasons
and Nandi is looking at an old scrapbook photo
of you lying next to me standing
in Uncle Albert's "especially tailored for"
she'll ask "who was that man sleeping"
and I'll say "is-is that man. Now, grab your shoes and the
purple jacket"

And then we'll visit 1045 Bells Mill Road
So she can feel the dirt underneath
The house with the big "A" on the front
That you and Granny's thumbless hands built.
And she'll look at her nails and say "ugh, can we go. It's
Chilly"
And I'll remember how, when Albert passed, you gave
Daddy
His "made in Hong Kong," so I could be warm
"up there near Roanoke with all them cold folks"

Behind your house
We will go walking across the earth's cold floor
Past the chicken coop that is no longer there
And I'll stop suddenly and tell her "shhh"
And she'll ask "what are you listenin' for"
And I'll say "listenin' to-dinner"
And with your big eyes she'll look at me strange
for a cold minute
Until I tell her the stories
Of how you broke bread with those chickens
Fattening them until
Granny cracked their necks and fried their legs

And again she'll say "ugh"
And then I'll show her the new Masonic Lodge
Which used to be the old Masonic Lodge
Which used to be the meeting place for those
Angry negro folks you would hear walking back from church
Preaching about taking us back to Africa.
And she'll ask, "did he go with them?"
And I'll smile and rub her head
The way your son used to rub mine
When I made him smile

And then, when we arrive at your gravesite
Down the street from Mount Lebanon Baptist
I'll jump out the car and open her door
And she'll frown and say "I can do it myself"
And I'll remember watching you
Open Granny's door,
Even when she told you
She could do it herself.

And when we kneel down beside you
To talk of ole' times
And pray for new ones
Her memory will rekindle
Even though she only met you twice
And she will joyfully ask,
As if someone long gone has come home
"was he my granddaddy too,"
and I'll smile again, my tears frozen in the winter air,
and tell her "is-is my granddaddy"

And then I'll stand up thinking that
I've showed her enough of you
To last another twenty seasons and
She'll grab my hand real tight

Like she's remembering something
And say "I like your coat, Daddy,"
And then I'll pick her up

Like you used to do me when I was six
And warmed your heart
Inside the car
We will drive back across the earth's cold floor
Back past the church
Back past the chickens
Back past the house with the big "A" on the front of the
house
Back past the scrapbook
Back to the photo
And while I'm remembering
She'll say "what are you thinking on?"
And I'll say "about-"
Thinking about
That strange white-robed man in the picture-
The one who kept calling you "Mr." instead of "Deacon"
The one who spoke at your funeral
About
How brave and wonderful you were
All the while never mentioning a word
About
Marcus Garvey
or Uncle Albert's coat

(1998)

ACTS OF LOVE

You never know he loves you
You overhear that he works like a slave
And that freedom is expensive
So you pay the price

There are no hot dogs and soda pop summers
Because there are no baseball games
Your tongue is not sweet on cotton candy
Because there are no moonlit carnivals

Time is money, smiles are seldom
Home is serious business
With little time for little things like
Card games and ping-pong and talking

Conversations become instructions:
Write all messages here
Clean the gutters as such
Mow the lawn like this

You crave his touch
Some small ritual of precious contact
Perhaps a drop of water in noonday heat
Even a forehead scratch would do

You never know he loves you
You overhear that he works like a slave
And that freedom is expensive
So you pay the price

Family meetings become trials:
Who took this message? Guilty

Why isn't the grass cut? Guilty
Did you finish up on the roof? Guilty

You never hear he loves you
Even in the car
Engine battling the hum of silence
Questions you're afraid to ask

Then one day in your Sunday proper
His sermon ended, the pews empty
You shadow his stillness
Hoping for some movement on this desert island

You look up into blinding sun
Sweat clings to high mountain
His face, a golden moon, now beams
His hands, spring rain drizzling scalp

And then you know.

(2005)

A LETTER TO MY DAUGHTER

August 18, 2009

Dear Nandi,

Yesterday, on the long drive to campus, I kept looking in the rear view mirror. No one was tailgating me, there weren't any cops, and the road was empty, but for some reason I found myself glancing behind me more than usual. It occurs to me, a day later, that while we were surely headed forward, moving ahead, I found it soothing to look back on the past 18 years. I suppose that in life it is important to remember where you've been, as you move ahead. These are just a few of things I remember about our past young lady. Things that I hope you will carry with you--as lessons, as reminders, as guides.

1. I never went to college parties. And you shouldn't either.

2. The first four years of your life, we lived in close to five different cities. You were a real trooper, adapting to the different areas and communities. And, when your mother and I divorced, you handled it better than most children do. Better than I would have. In fact, when I was older than you, my parents announced that they were separating, and I cried and begged and pleaded for them to work it out. And, they did. And, if they hadn't I would have been a wreck. Nandi, since the beginning, you have been a strong woman. You bounce back. You manage expectations well. You adjust. You will need this during the next four years, as this is probably the biggest life change you will encounter. So, embrace

it. Run circles around yet another city in your life. Keep doing what you've been doing since you were a baby.

3. Of course, I know you are a sensitive little lady, and I know that even though you've handled lots of challenges in your life brilliantly. But, I also know that you keep some things inside. A little of that is okay. A lot, not so okay. Nandi, if you ever feel like the pieces of the puzzle don't fit, your world is too unpleasant, and the sky is crashing, talk to someone. Talk to me. Talk to your God. Talk to your teacher. Talk to the girl at Starbucks. Talk to a therapist. Talk to someone. See, sometimes, sharing offers focus, and listening is an act of love that can renew your spirit.

4. One month into your mother's pregnancy, I saw you in a dream. Vividly. I saw your nose, eyes, skin. You were as clear as spring water. I was 22, with no idea how to be a father, and a little afraid I might add. But, after the dream, I was thrilled, gung-ho, quite excited about your joining us. Eight months later, in the delivery room, I guess I went overboard, videotaping the whole thing. I was just so filled with joy at the opportunity to meet and help raise you. I told myself that when you went to college, I would let you watch the video. I thought it would be one of those movie-moments that we could share together. Well, I went back to look at a little of it, and I stopped after a few seconds. I realized that this is one of those rare moments in our history that I want to remember as is. Knowing is great, but I'd rather hold on to the feeling.

5. After the divorce, you came to stay with me every other weekend. Back in those days as a starving artist, I didn't have a lot of material things. I had a few books, poems, and lots of love for you. Whenever you'd come visit, you'd always say things like "I like your hat, daddy," or "I like

your coat, daddy." It was the most wonderful feeling in the world each time you uttered those sentiments. It made me feel on top of the world, and I thank you for that. Nandi, as you encounter people in life, whether it's your professor or the guy mowing the lawn, your roommate or the cafeteria aide, always share positive sentiments with them. You don't know what's going on in their life, good or bad, but a few wonderful words can make someone feel brighter, can make a lonely poet forget about the bus fare he doesn't have.

6. FYI, I never went to parties in college. I studied all the time.

7. Speaking of college, junior year I took a sociology class. I loved the class. And the teacher. I just never went to class. I did the papers--on issues that I was interested in. And skipped the tests. Needless to say, I flunked the final. Now, when grades came, I was totally expecting an "F." It just so happened, that junior year was my "radical" year. It was the year I organized anti-apartheid rallies on campus, held protests in the snow, and generally worked day and night to make conditions better for minority groups. So, I was very active on campus, just not attending too many classes. So, when the grades came out, my sociology professor had given me a C+. He explained that while most of the students were learning about Minority Group Relations in his class, I was out learning about it and putting it into practice in a real world situation, and he admired that. Okay, first, I am not saying you should skip classes. That would be a mistake (and I would have to cut off your allowance--SMILE), but I think college is about learning in and out of the classroom. Become involved Nandi. Bridge that gap between knowledge and experience.

8. Okay, so I went to one party in college. It was a local weekly dance contest, at the Marriott. Started at 11:00 pm on Friday nights. I'd won a couple Fridays, and your uncle Marshall won a few Fridays also. Well, one Friday night they had the final competition, and Marshall and I, and are partners went head to head. I should have won, but Marshall started doing some combination of the Reebok and the Jerk (Google it). And, losing was a terrible experience for me. Which is the point, that if you never go to parties and dance contests Nandi, you will never lose. So don't go to any parties.

9. Honesty. Rule #1 in life. Never lie. (unless you're telling your first child you didn't go to parties in college. That is okay.) Your reputation is how folks know and respect you Nandi. First and foremost, be an honest and trustworthy person, and not only will others feel good about you, but you will feel good about yourself. Speaking of which, please sign the form that says I can view your grades at the end of each semester.

10. Friendship. Rule #2 in life. You attract what you are. When you look in your rear view mirror, do you see the kinds of friendships that will last a lifetime? I suspect not. College is a place where all that changes. My best friend in life, the guy who beat me in the dance contest, I met the first day of college. If you want to meet good, honest, caring, friendly people, then be good, honest, caring and friendly from day one. It's as simple as that.

11. Here are some of the highlights of life with you, my dear:

The day you were born.
The day you bit the boy in preschool
The day my first book came out, with our photo on the cover

The day we sat outside in 100 degree weather selling books
The day you won the MLK historical essay contest
The day you walked down the aisle of my wedding
The day you announced you wanted to be a poet
The day we went to Kings Dominion with Marshall, Anita and her kids
The day you started high school
The day you started varsity volleyball as a freshman
The day you turned 16 and I showed up in the Limo
The day you came to live with me
The day during your junior year when you told us "I got this, school will be fine"
The day you opened the letter from NYU and it said you got a full scholarship to the Summer Program
The day you watched Samayah for the first time, and didn't drop her
The day you graduated cum laude
The day you got offered the full scholarship to College
The day I got the bill for $0
The day you walked up the hill to your dorm and never looked back

12. So, here we are, 18 years after The Dream. And, I find myself wanting to say something deep. To offer some glimpse of what the future will hold for you Nandi. And, the reality is, you don't need me to tell you what the future will hold, anymore than you needed me to videotape your birth. I'm the one looking back, trying to remember. You're on your way up the hill, In the dorm, up the stairs, to room 218. Looking forward. "I got this, Dad," is what I hear, and I believe that you do. I guess this is more about me. Wasn't it just a minute ago when we were walking to the tennis courts in Ashland, or swinging in the park in Norfolk, or singing some of our favorite made-up songs? Geesh, Nandi,

I miss you already! I miss the drama and your dynamic charm. I miss your attitude and your attention to family. I miss your fiery personality (just a little) and your focus on excellence. I know you're not gone, you're just in another city, and now I must learn to adapt and adjust. Don't worry though, "I think I got this..." Cheers!

Dad

PS. Your mother never partied either.

*T*S Eliot once said 'Immature poets imitate; mature poets steal.' My first teacher was my mother. She would often spoil my sulking with homemade lemonade and hilarious poemsongs that sent me howling with laughter. I fell in love with the power of her voice. Later, I would encounter teachers, librarians, poets, musicians-some through the pages of books, others firsthand, several in friendship-who would influence me, and my creative work. I am humbled by these folks who have helped shape this dance I do with words...I remember walking into an advanced poetry class as a college sophomore. The professor was a legendary and fiery poet. As a legendary (in my own mind) and fiery student leader, I naturally, challenged her every remark, critique, and edit with a poem that screamed 'rebel.' The poetry wasn't that good (and neither was my attitude), but I like to think that my intentions were honest. Authentic. I guess she did too, because over the years she would open many doors for me. And my poetry. She would teach my emphatic blackness that night often comes softly. Others would come around also, pushing and prodding, giving me the audacity to dream. To do the write thing. To squeeze that last bit of juice from the lemon. We must all raise a toast to those who wake us up. To the sweetness of life.

A NIKKI POEM

An Empty Page
An Honest Word
A Carpentered Verse
A Gemini Woman
A Sizzling Tongue
A Revered Wit
A Honeyed Hearth
A Black-eyed Pea
A Sacred Cow
A Night Wind
A Rainy Day
A Dahlia Blossom
A Re: Creation
A Radical Love
A Black Song
A Soft Black Song
A Nikki Poem

(2004)

TANKA

(FOR MAYA ANGELOU)

i hear freedom in
yr voice ancient as the African
song wading
water some sacred arpeggio
kissing memory

(2005)

AFTER READING E. ETHELBERT MILLER

I tried writing a yellow melon
And slicing through a sonnet
It's just that my lovers didn't make sense anymore
And my poems were full of questions

Do dictators sleep?
Where are the night poems?
How do we promise?
We don't make love, why?

It was as if my faith was flipped
Even the world seemed possible
And some beautiful laugh with no first name
Walked the night with a gal named Elegba

This was suddenly a beautiful place
Where everyone flirted with hope. And change
And in my little piece of sky
The people sang a boogie-woogie blues

And, best of all
They could fly,
and dance and dream
and eat and sleep (and make love too)
all at the same time
all
    at the
           same
time.

(2007)

KUPENDA 41

(FOR SONIA SANCHEZ)

essence magazine
ought to be renamed
something intimate
more fire i say
more rhythm i say
like the
singing coming off of drums
under a soprano sky
make it musical
make it personal sensual even
meaning
a blue black woman
with a baaaaaad tongue
and a forever flame
who looks good too
I say call it
Sonia I Say
Call her Sonia Yeah!

(2000)

AFTER LISTENING TO
BEWARE THE SHORT HAIR GIRL

i fell asleep chanting
your song hot as summer
sand some sweet soprano
skipping across the sun
dancing between the stars
night woman u own me
yr music tattooed
on my spirit etched in the
the memory
of two thousand seasons
i dream yr body
of music
my midnight Holiday
nightwoman u own me
yr a capella a big, wide grin
the words like
school children chasing Friday or
church folk eating Sunday
this is how i want to live
swimming in soul
inside
yr soft, strong sound
can u feel me humming along
nightwoman?
last night
i fell asleep chanting yr song
and woke up with jazz
on my tongue

(2007)

DRIVE

(FOR DR. JULIANNE MALVEAUX, ON THE OCCASION
OF HER APPOINTMENT AS THE 15TH PRESIDENT OF
BENNETT COLLEGE FOR WOMEN. READ AT ANNIE
MERNER PFEIFFER CHAPEL DURING THE INAUGURAL
CONCERT, MARCH 29, 2008)

How does a woman get to work?
Does she point towards freedom,
walk towards justice?
stepping sharply, tapping brilliance
with feet that don't even belong here

Does she dance towards destiny?
with love draped over her shoulder
like sacks of summer cotton?

When our young women are in crisis *From Dusk to Dawn*
When our scholars are *In Search of our Mother's Gardens*
When a sister is called to work at Bennett
Maybe she just Drives….

Like Nzingha's Army crossing over and Harriet Stealing a
way
Drive(Sister)
Like Faye Robinson Singing with a sword in her hand
Drive(Sister)
Like Mary McLeod Bethune Oh, My good Lord,
showing us the way
Drive(Sister)
Like Maya Blowing her sweet trumpet and Sadie Tanner
Alexander
Climbing Jacob's ladder
Drive(Sister)
Like Phyllis Wallace and Willa Player

Like Marian Anderson and Sonia Sanchez
Like Dorothy Height Marching 'round Selma
under a soprano sky
Just Drive(Sister)

And when you get sick and tired
Of being sick and tired (and you will)
Pull over
park yourself under the baobab tree
enfold yourself in kente
enjoy a slice of peace
watch the spirit fill you up
listen to the new wheels a turning
and with each revolution
you'll keep driving
our women
to their destinies
keep driving our women
to wealth and happiness
keep driving our women
towards freedom

With your silver smile and crystal gait
our women will look to you
and know their beautiful black selves: So
Keep Working Sister
Keep Walking Sister
Keep Pointing Sister
Keep Dancing Sister
Keep Driving Sister
'cause we are ready to ride!

(2007)

FLY GIRL

(FOR BESSIE COLEMAN)

she is dawn wind
                blazing
through white clouds
sucking mist
criss
    crossing
zig
    zagging
            soaring
into sun rise
like two lovers
crowding morning
she is amber sun
in olive drab khakis
and taut jacket
                sweeping
the blue, hot, moist air
a little bird hops
on her wing
reminding us that
nobody
owns the sky

(2005)

A BORROWED POEM

(ON THE OCCASION OF THE DEDICATION OF THE DR.
CLARENCE V. CUFFEE COMMUNITY CENTER AND LIBRARY,
CHESAPEAKE, VIRGINIA. READ AT THE DEDICATION
CEREMONY, FEBRUARY 10, 2007

In the twilight of youth
So much is taken for granted
That you are a testament to spirit
That you can rise above the stars
And somewhere between the pages of truth
You will dare to dream about becoming
And skating on the heels of history
You will dare to dream of your future
When the world is afraid of change
You will dare to dream of leading
When normal wears heavy like a ship's anchor
You will dare to dream of living different
Your words will touch and grab
Scream and whisper
Struggle and fight
Love and learn
Dream and dare
To be young
To be proud
To be new
To be free
To sail to success
So when the stars come out to dance
What a delight it will be
To realize that all the time
They were within your reach

Note: Poem contains excerpts of a poem written by the former City
Manager of Chesapeake, VA Dr. Clarence V. Cuffee (1945-2005)

(2007)

FOR NIKKI GIOVANNI

My friend, if you were a song
I'd call you jazz

Clap for you
Snap to you

Sing to you
Swing with you

I'd color you Ellington
Elegant and Essential in my life

(2008)

A POEM COMMEMORATING THE INAUGURATION OF BARACKOBAMA, THE 44TH PRESIDENT OF THE UNITED STATES, & THE 80TH BIRTHDAY OF DR. MARTIN LUTHER KING, JR.

(READ AT THE HISTORIC INAUGURAL BALL, JANUARY 19, 2009, AT THE HISTORICAL SOCIETY OF WASHINGTON, DC)

How do you write an American poem?
A red, white, and weary blues poem
A poem filled with change, like a bag of pennies

in your grandmother's chimney poem
An American poem, with one hand holding history
and the other clinching vision

A borrowed poem
that pays us back by any means necessary poem
How do you write an American poem?

one with baggage like some Pullman Porter poem
A rainbow wrapped in chains untenable poem
A dark and deadly middle passage unspeakable poem

A this is your land until we took it indigenous poem
A we are not enemies, but friends unguarded poem
A we all fought to save an imperfect Union audacious
poem

A we ought to be free and independent poem
A surviving Jim Crow reconstruction poem

A where do we go from here renaissance poem
A return to copper sun Heritage poem

How do you write and American poem?
A we shall not be moved invincible poem
A four girls down south massacred poem
A where do we go from there militant poem
A black as the night is beautiful poem
A why we can't wait community poem
A why we don't have to unbelievable poem
that swims across the river of our imagination poem
and takes us to the majestic shores of the promised land
poem

How do you write an American poem?
A few folks still won't get the change memo unfortunate
poem

A that's okay, because humanity I love you undeniable
poem
A we support the troops, not the trauma poem
A life, liberty and the pursuit of a joyful noise incredible
poem

A new face for our country-unending poem
A listen can't you hear the ancestors singing unbending
poem.
A Great day! Great day, the righteous marching poem

A shine your light on the world,
shine your light for the world to see poem
And don't stop 'til the break of dawn jubilee poem

A new birth of freedom revealed poem
A tunnel of hope to heal poem
A long-time coming not so unreal poem
A sophisticated and unflappable poem
A we real cool as a pint of joy poem
A the children now know their reach is unlimited poem

How do you write an American poem
that has not been written yet?
With sacred honor and the audacity to dream.

(2009)

1988: I attended a master writing class in Atlanta, taught by creative luminaries like Bill Duke, Cicely Tyson, Douglass Turner Ward, and Spike Lee. There were about 10 of us-college students-from around the country selected for the program. Several are now professional writers, some actors Off-Broadway, one even a television star. My most vivid memory of this awesome experience is me sharing a poem-about some trite concern-and proudly boasting that I was a Writer (capital W intentional), and the playwright Charles Fuller asking me had I written anything meaningful? More importantly, had I finished anything? Then me not feeling so awesome anymore. 1992: It's Your Mug was a coffeehouse on P Street in Georgetown (DC) that turned into a poetry church on Wednesday Night. Many names, small and big, took communion at those teeming open mics. There was a kid, one Wednesday, who was halfway through a trite poem about...well, let's just say this poem was foul-mouthed and simply looking for attention. It was offensive, abusive, and probably needed to be tried and jailed. While the faithful congregation sat appalled, and silent, I suddenly became the judge delivering a sermon. "Cut!" I yelled. He stopped. Everyone looked. Perplexed. At me. At him. "That's enough," I explained. Later, two poets told me that what I'd done wasn't cool, and what was I thinking by disrespecting the mic. I thought of Charles Fuller. 'Write a poem that cooks,' I mumbled, which confused them even more.

DANCING NAKED ON THE FLOOR

write a poem with tension...like some baptist church split...let it walk a tightrope...between congregation one...and congregation two...write a poem that finishes school...a magna cum laude poem...let it be momentous...learn something meaningful...share something significant...write a poem that looks good... not homely or swaybacked...give it posture, poise and profile...turn our heads when it walks by...stomp our feet when it smiles...on some superficial level...make us want to marry it or at least...remember its name the next morning...write a poem that works...write a poem that works...has a job and does it...promptly...follows rules and responsibilities...gets a raise or at least a head nod... and when it's not feeling well...give it sense enough to call in sick...and not waste our time with unmet expectations... write a poem that has a family...not some single life of one-night stands...i mean your poem should be in a serious relationship...let it commit to something...move beyond soap opera sex...let it be passionate...about something... and if it gets excited...if it just has to get physical...let it be in the privacy of it's own beautiful mind....cause we can watch cable at home...write a poem that travels...gets outside of your cramped apartment...leaves all that tired baggage...and catches a plane somewhere...takes us on a journey to an imagination... spawned not by television and film...but one that has been somewhere we haven't... write a poem that reads...please...write...a...poem... that...reads...more than headlines and sitcom credits...a cultured poem...write a poem that knows how to talk... not some misbehaving foul-mouth looking for attention... an eloquent poem...write a poem that dances...wild and free...naked on the floor...a gutsy poem...write a poem that cooks...i mean it ain't got to bake a cake...

but at least know the ingredients...write a poem that exercises...i mean cycling is not required...but steps never hurt nobody...write a poem that runs for office...i mean it ain't got to win...but at least campaign...get a clue poets...write a poem with an inkling of suspicion...i mean it ain't got to solve a crime...but let it at least offer a tip...write a poem that is contagious...write a poem that is contagious...write a poem that is contagious...let it inspire...make us...want to write a poem...about how brilliant...and breathtaking...and tragic...and hopeful... life is.

(2004)

OUR WOMEN

Women
Our women
Not like we own you
Like you are the only women for us
We seek life
Our women black/hold on to us
Like sunset caressing midnight
Like midnight entering sunrise
Like sunrise giving birth to daylight
Sista you shine
Sista you mine
Not like I own you
Like I dig you
My precious black gold
And while it may be counterrevolutionary
You my diamond mine
My mind
Mine. Dig? You
My woman
Our women
Black and naturally
Smooth and Black
And vigorous and Black
And practical and Black
Intellectual and Black
And naturally
You fine
Our women
Dark-soiled earth
Seed planted in you
Bring life forth
Bring life force
Our women Black

Morning mint-flavored
Coffee brown-Black
Copper shining amber
Sun-burned Black
Ochre khaki rust
Rising high yellow Black
Evening coal-sabled
Chestnuts roasting Black
Late night sun-setting
Pitch jet Black
Spadiceous
Stramineous
and castaneous
Our women Black
and naturally
We are your men

(1993)

WHEN

the world is not so beautiful
the flowers waste water

the women can no longer find their song
the children refuse to play

there are no men to teach to love
the ground inside collapses

the coldest winter screams
the summer burns red

the sea is full of blues
and the sky opens up

At least I'll have poetry
a gathering of words

a get-together of emotions
a font of ideas

hope with wings
poems that fly

(2009)

MEMO TO COMPANY PRESIDENT

today
let us toast
i have decided
to ask for a pay decrease
i know it sounds strange
but i no longer want that promotion
or the vacant office
sick leave, pointless
my cabinets are well-stocked with echinacea
plus, i want to be a team player
in fact, i am returning my comp time
from now on, i will work weekends (for free)
there were no bonuses this year (for us)
but do know that, theoretically, i am giving that back
too

see, i now realize
that it would be healthier
if i were miserable
on purpose
rather than continue working in earnest
while
corporate greed and
calculated lies
shatter your pledge
of loyalty

(2004)

SOUL ON FIRE
(A POEMSONG)

And the Sun God said "that's hip"
And it was and she was too
I mean she was so hip she was
Double hip like
When she sat down she was
Still standing like
Some ole' Egyptian Queen
From way back from way way
Black jack you diggin' it
I mean sister was
Nefertiti livin' in your neighborhood
Sheba walkin' down your street or
If you was real lucky
Cleopatra chillin' at your crib
I mean sister was
So fly
And she kept getting flyer
Flyer and flyer
And I couldn't even breathe
Her air
On account of
My soul was on fire

And the Sun God said "that's cool"
And it was and she was too
I mean sister was so cool
She even taught white folks how to dance
Now that's cool she was
Geographically cool
Living bi-coolstal
Somewhere between hot and cold
Even her temper was lukewarm

Like an infant I was a newcomer and
She my coolcomer always on time
Never late so cool
The clocks stopped she was
Stopwatch cool
Brothers would stop and watch
And watch and stop
But failed to jock
Thought she was too hot
Not knowing her was merely cool-hot
But I knew cause I was cool too
So I walked to her cool
On time with my line
Say sista, you cool
And I'm cool
So why don't we just cool out together-
But of course my cool was too late
Cause by then she was just chillin'
But she was still fly
And she kept getting flyer
Flyer and flyer and
I kept climbing higher
Higher and higer
And I still couldn't breathe
Her air
On account of
My soul was on fire

And the Sun God said "that's deep"
And it was and she was too
I mean sister was so deep
When she looked up she saw her back
Now that's deep even her conversations
Were deep orgasmically tripping me
Into a black hole of her words
Like

Hip
Cool
and *Na Kupenda Sana,* baby-
You can't get deeper than that
She was deep like Atlantis
I mean you knew she was there
But you just couldn't touch her
But I could cause I was deep too
Like a crescendo
on the rise
Climbing high so high so fly
So you ask what her name is-
Well if you was hip to her cool
Then you wouldn't have to ask
So it must be too deep for you but
I tell you this
She was so fly
So fly
So fly
And she kept getting flyer
Flyer and flyer
I kept climbing higher
Higher and higher
And I still couldn't breathe
Her air but
Thank God
My soul was on fire

(1995)

RENGA

(WHY BLACK FOLKS DON'T TIP)

it has something to
do with the way you sling our
brand new luggage
onto dirt-caked curbs like rank
red meat for some mangy dog

or, perhaps

it's because we have
glimpsed snow in august more
than we've seen you
even though we pleaded for
refills thirty minutes ago

then again

it cd be that yr
eyes reveal a prophecy
we ache to fulfill

maybe it's as simple as

we built this rich country and
you refused to pay. no mules
no land, plain stiffed us
so just be happy we're
paying the damn bill

(2005)

IM(US) BE CRAZY

(OR, A POEM ABOUT THE NUMBER OF TIMES THE H-WORD
HAS BEEN REFERENCED IN HIP HOP MUSIC, BUT WE CAN'T
SAY JESUS IN SCHOOL. GOD HELP US)

My friend calls in an uproar
Asks me what do I think?
I tell her I don't.
We like the sound she makes
The hiss of asses jiggling
The hint of bad in her air
She is a good person
Who just sings along
while her children laugh
and play
and listen

It occurs to me
That when someone, somewhere says something stupid,
hurtful,
crushing,
When the world feels ugly
Poets should make it beautiful again, or at least keep it
honest:
Enron could have used a poet.
Bush needs a black poet, or two, in the White House
All week I have waited for a call from MSNBC:
We need a poem, we have turmoil here,
Advertisers are jumping ship, our world is collapsing
Al Roker is not eating.
We have called the preachers
They are praying for us
We have even called Dave Chapelle
He tells us not to worry,
just put a beat behind it, and they will be happy again
I say, we need a poem.

There is a man on the train
Sitting across from me
His feet flirt with the floor
His pale hands unravel the news
But what has my attention
Is his voice, a booming brew
Of hoots, snorts, and cackles.
He is talking with the woman next to him.
Man: What's the big deal?
Woman: It was degrading and demeaning
Man: Come on, Ho is a part of the vernacular
and then comes his cackle,
and my rage
and, alas the poem:

In America, the greatest reward for
odious language,
and wanton behavior,
is to have young people
call you cool,
cop your album,
while tuning in to
your reality show
Should Imus be fired?
if we fire Jay-Z
if we fire Kanye
if we fire Eminem
if we fire Aaron McGruder
if we fire Quentin Tarantino
if we fire Jamie Foxx
if we fire Samuel Jackson
if we fire LL
when we fire Chris Rock
if we fire (fill in the blank)
Then, yeah, maybe he should.
then, maybe

poets won't be the only ones
unafraid of truth
won't be the only ones
willing to stop singing
the same sad songs.

(2007)

BETTY

my Betty
lives
downstairs
in 1b
looks 38
is 83
and fine
like old wine
she steps out
of virginia's dew
breathin'
newport air
on her way
upstairs
to loan me
bread
for my french toast
i thank her with a hug
she holds on tight like
it is her last slice
i hope it isn't
because early mornings
wouldn't be the same
without my french toast/no
they just wouldn't be the same

(1995)

DADDY

Wednesday nights don't make me feel too good. I toss and turn in my bed thinking of Thursday morning. The day I gotta get up extra early to hear momma scream "take out the trash boy." So, I get up and put on whatever is lying on the floor next to me that I was supposed to put in the hamper yesterday. Then I put on my hat. Walking through the house is always fun. I can stop by the kitchen and steal some of the cake that momma told us not to touch. It's a good kind of feeling to be the only one up, get some milk, and watch all the ladies on TV try to lose weight. Then I get some orange juice. Standing in the doorway, I see momma. In my mind. With her belt. I quickly remember that I'm supposed to take out all the trash in the house. And anything else I see lying around. So then I finally get all the bags together and take out all the trash. Heading back into the house, I always have this feeling that I've forgotten something. And then I think of Daddy.

(1989)

HOW WE LOVE

it does not take
a math genius
to understand that
when you subtract
a man
from the equation
what remains
is negative

no matter
how many ways
you divide
the responsibility of
family
once you factor in
a manchild
pining for a fraction
of love
his future seldom
adds up

this problem
cannot be solved
by theorems and what ifs
this problem, the sum total
of our actions
leaves our children questioning
and if we knew the answers
the numbers would show it
and the evening news would not

perhaps, we need a new formula
one that will

extract our roots
find the most common denominator
prove beyond words
that a village does indeed
raise a child
and that we can count
on you
the women and
the menblack

(2005)

JUST US

Black poems will
Feed black minds but
Who will put chakula
Into the children's bellies
And make them full with nourishment

Black poems will
Cleanse black souls but
Who will give proper attention
To women hungry for time
And respect

Black poems will
Love thin sheets of white paper but
Who will develop proud black youth
Who will nurture thick black hearts
Who will create strong black families

It must be us
Just us

(1994)

LIFE
(FOR PROFESSOR DERRICK BELL)

This morning
I woke to find

Termites
Eating away at

My home
My friends assured me that

The good liberal ones
Were not involved

(1993)

HEROES, GODS, AND ME

"You guys," Miss Friendly says, (speaking to all of us)
"can be anything you want," as

she points to our 'Wall of Achievement:'
Shakespeare, Kennedy, King, and other

great men, with even greater dreams.
She smiles. "Throughout mankind, Gods

and heroes like Napoleon, Hercules, (& Rocky?)
have won battles, ruled worlds, saved

humanity." She asks each of us about our future plans.
When she reaches me, I search for a picture. "What about

you Annie," she says, still smiling, "who do you want to
become?"And even though I'm still a kid (who likes dolls

and pink) I know that I don't want to become like Miss
Friendly, some missing portrait on the wall of history.

(2006)

ON BEING ASKED BY A MIDDLE SCHOOL STUDENT "WAS NIKKI GIOVANNI MARRIED TO TUPAC?"

Cora
wants
to
know
is the Sun a woman
and if so
who
is
her
husband?
i will tell her
that
Astronomy is not my favorite subject
but, I do know a few poems
who have dated
and every now and then
there is talk of marriage
because love
is a strange and funny thing
i will tell her
that
sometimes
the question is much
more interesting
than the
answer

(2007)

EBONY IMAGES

ebony
trapped
dark black
and lovely
brown mocha
brown black
jumpin double
black brown
night black
outta sight black
so black
purple black
blue black
black blue
black black
brown smoked
Morrocan black
yellow black
mellow yellow
black brown
positive
chocolate
brown black
free
black
images

(1987)

WHERE DO WE GO FROM HERE?

wrap yourself in a mountain of prayer
there is no more comfort in speech
and protest proves no match for line items

so what is to be said to the sons
and daughters of freedom?
that oil and ego trump blood and ethos?

surely there can be no consolation
for the mass leaving
no spring

for the blizzard of death returning
only a mother's face
fairway green with hope

that white men will transform
the blazing colors of our rainbow
and learn to love

themselves
that America will sing victory and
finally win this war against

itself

(2004)

BUCK AND WING/THE FLOW

These are not times for poets
Iambic pentameters
Will not/wake up/the job mar/ket
Alliteration
Cannot convince corporate capitalists
To consider your competence
Metaphors
Will not move the sun
And you won't own the night
(or your house)
even your unrhymed
haiku are longer than the
next temp assignment
because the only full-time jobs
are in the army reserves
for the hopeless young
forced to star in the latest reality show
Who wants to die

These are not times for poets
Stock options are not available
For builders of words
401ks do not exist for literary photographers
of pain and hope
there are no benefits for those
who tell the truth about
unfair housing and Iraq
and second-hand smoke and
Other reasons to riot

These are not times for poets
Health care is not covered
Under the starving artist plan

Try not to smile in front of others
Especially on interviews
Because dentists don't accept
Concise wordplay as payment
And yes God is good
And Jesus loves you but
Hospitals get real inhospitable
If your Cross ain't Blue

These are not times for poets
There are no six-figure advances for
Singers of sonnets and sestinas
There are not best picture awards
For your moving words
No dave chapelle money
For your witty canto
Hollywood has closed its doors to free verse
Because good costs
And it's cheaper to
Stare blankly into
The coffers of mediocrity
Especially when cialis and viagra
Are footing the bill
And still we can't go on like this forever

These are not times for poets
Who wander without tradition
Who fight without armor

These are not times for poets
Whose pages are filled with latchkey words
And blanked vision

These are not times for poets
That race around tenured tracks
Clique in tow

Who publish and perish
Because nobody reads their poems
(not even their own mamas)

These are not times for poets who
Love freedom more
Than they love applause
Calling all strong poets
Whose word exercise
Whose stanzas bench press our burdens
Whose poems lift the weight
Off our world
And put it in a better place.

(2004)

*W*e lived in Morningside Heights first. 121st and Amsterdam. Then Brooklyn. Crown Heights. I was three-years-old when my parents took me to The East. Founded in 1969 by a friend of my father's, Jitu Weusi, The East was located in the heart of Bedford-Stuyvesant. It was a black cultural center where musicians, poets, and artists performed and held workshops. Events held at The East were no small matters. It was widely known for drawing crowds of thousands to hear lectures by H. Rap Brown, and KwameTure (Stokely Carmichael), among others. Weekly music performances included local artists and internationally-recognized jazz greats including Max Roach, Randy Weston and Betty Carter. By the time I was ten, The East would become a weekend haunt of my parents, and I was right there with them—at the the epicenter of black thought and performance. Listening to the seductive wit and wisdom of Amiri Baraka, Haki Madhubuti, Sonia Sanchez and other Black Arts Poets. Catching glimpses of lovers laughing and learning. Clutching and kissing. This is what I remember most about The East: Sensuality greeted you at the front door, and it held your hand (tight) the whole night. It would be much later before I would hold a woman's hand. Before I would make a lover laugh. Before I would find poems that danced naked. But when I did, I would find them in the strangest places...

HAIKU

i knead you, feel you
shaping, rising, moist and warm
slowly coming round

(2009)

KUPENDA 96

i find poems
in the strangest
places between
your legs is
a pantoum
dying
to be penned
is a verse
waiting
to be freed

(2008)

A THOUGHT

yr breasts
are couplets

i like
to rhyme

all the
tme

(2007)

KUPENDA 19

lips like yours
ought to be worshipped
see, i ain't never been
too religious
but you can baptize me
anytime

(1994)

WHY I LIKE THE POST OFFICE

once
i was
yr stamp
firm and moist
to touch
then i was
the letter
inside
your box
that always
came (priority)
do you remember
the way
you
enveloped me
the way yr tongue
sealed my package
I wonder
can
you
still
taste
me?

(2008)

HAIKU

i like being your
apple, the way you peel me
get under my skin

(2008)

HAIKU

nectarine lady
ripe and red to my touch
fresh and sweet in my mouth

(2009)

KUPENDA 15

i am a
dawn ocean
thrusting my
midnight waves
onto yr
sandy shore
until yr tide
comes
in

(1993)

YOU MAKE ME WANT TO

mix citrus and melon drink

you in the morning pluck
your tiny seeds at

night seeing you was a
reminder that my arms still

reach around your
world I have not forgotten

that loving you was
nice and sweet but now I must learn to

remember that being a part of
you somehow makes up for

never being inside of
you

(1999)

NEGRIL, JAMAICA

I will sip the limeade
while you jerk the chicken
Later, we will sunbathe
on the deck
before the night comes
and we can be newlyweds
all over again

(2000)

HAIKU

if i pull your cork
will you satisfy my thirst,
let me drink you in?

(2007)

HAIKU

your wet legs on my
glass pressing for a sweet taste
and making me blush

(2007)

KUPENDA 49

i have heard Fuji
roar with laughter
(at least thrice)
tasted morning dew
on trembling bush
hootchy-kootchied on the wing
of fireflies stealing night
can we please go to sleep now?

(2005)

HAIKU

if i am your heart
imagine me inside
beating, pumping, loving

(2006)

BONUS POEMS

It was national poetry month 2012, and I wanted to do something fun and poetic and sensual and humorous. On Facebook. I didn't outline it, or brainstorm, I just started writing. What developed was a narrative about a man and a woman. I posted one poem and the response was encouraging. So I wrote another. Before I knew it folks were asking for the next one. This is not autobiographical, though I did draw from some pretty memorable experiences in college, and more recently, in Africa. I include it here, as a sort of bonus series of poems—or hidden verse, as it were—to this revised paperback edition of my selected poems. I may pick it back up at some point and explore this relationship. For now, enjoy and thanks for the support. Tchau!

A SHORT STORY IN VERSE

1.

on the way home
they argue

like Africans
in traffic

he fumes
the way she melted

like Sub-saharan Shea butter
when Claude, the painter

bragged about the time
he ran into

Alice Walker
after making love

behind a bouquiniste
on the Seine

later, in bed
his heart is muted

their backs
two gridlocked bumpers

kissing
under quiet stars

he has almost said something
sixteen times

When she finally figures out how to tell him
that while bald frenchmen and colors may excite her

she is a word woman first
she wants to be written, wholly and solely, by a poet

she rubs his scalp
and sings like someone in love

the way
she sprinkles

jazz
in his ear

tempts
his familiar

turns him
around

2.

the next day
curled up
in the couch
watching baseball
after dinner
she says she
has the urge
to pitch you
let you hit

it out of the park.
But first
go do the dishes.

3.

From the kitchen
he glimpes her calf
the left one
dangling
a smooth, satisfying curve
a trumpet
blowing his mind.

He wants her.

The last black pot glistens
Its lid a sweet silver flash
He holds the fork like a bedtime ritual
and carefully bathes each tine.
You see, the dishwasher is too loud
plus, he gets to listen to Jazz.

When he is almost finished
ready to round the bases
he hears the sea
A wave of salt and sorrow
and knows
she is watching the News. again.
something about a boy and Skittles
and rain. and blood. and the weight
of being black.

Before there is ocean
he turns down Dexter Gordon

and hollers:

You know its national poetry month, right?
Maybe, tonight I'll pen a pantoum.

she laughs
and flips the channel
it lands on Jeopardy
the category
Math:

what is:
I want more
I want the whole geometry of you
connect me with those lines
of leg and toe, elbow and neck
he says
to himself.

The last dish cleaned
He moves to her.
Lifts.
Carries.
Places.
Peels off her shiny stockings
This is where I want to be, he thinks.
But right before he can divide her
above the unpredictable sound of Miles
he hears
the complexity of their love
he hears
the sweet thunder that is life
he hears
out of nowhere

"I'm leaving."

4.

they met
in college
at a gospel
barbecue

he was reciting
a poem
about how
you should never
mix citrus fruits
with melons

she was praise dancing
carrying
a cracked claw
like a torch
with a big chunk of crab
blazing in the air

for a year, all they did
was smile
each day
at 7:30
in line
for breakfast.
today was different.

"you're the poet,"
came a voice
from behind
his chair

he swallowed
because spitting

watermelon seeds
was not an option

"come with me,
I want to show you
something," she said
grabbing his sticky hand
he followed, of course
eyeing her dancer legs
those calves
will be the end
of me, he thought

the next weekend
she invited him
to see Spandau Ballet:

when he explained
that he loved to dance,
but he just wasn't
into ballet, and would
she mind if they just
caught Footloose
at the Lyric
she kissed him
on the cheek
like Mrs. Cuffee did
when he volunteered
to trim her hedges
then pulled out
his mother's
kitchen scissors.

before the movie
he made her dinner:
Rice. Chicken. Broccoli.

but, it was the homemade rolls
and the listening to Marvin
that molded her heart
and shaped her love
that made her legs rise
like two piccolo trumpets
dancing naked
under the moon

they never made it
to the Lyric

a week later
she moved in
with her Bible,
her soft-rock CDs,
and a sweet-smelling
Orange Blossom
that never fully
bloomed.

5.

In the first week their sizzle
was thundering. After he
introduced her to Fela

she taught him the secret to
a good omelet: Chili
powder. They watched St. Elmo's

Fire three times, overslept twice
The way she woke him each day
was epic and electric.

6.

Before she goes
they make love
in the 9th inning
to the sound
of a runner
stealing home

ABOUT KWAME ALEXANDER

Kwame Alexander is an award-winning poet, children's book author, playwright, producer, and the author of fourteen books including Crush: Love Poems for Teenagers, and a children's picture book, Acoustic Rooster and His Barnyard Band (A 2012 NAACP Image Award Nominee). His first novel will be published by HarperCollins in 2013. Since 2006, Kwame's Book-in-a-day writing & publishing program for middle and high school students has created more than 2500 student authors in 50 schools across the U.S., and in Canada and the Caribbean. Kwame regularly conducts creative writing workshops and performances in middle and high schools. Most recently, he served as Guest Author for the Grand Cayman Libraries Summer Reading Programme, Poet-in-Residence at Foxcroft Girls Boarding School in Virginia, and Poet-in-Residence for Loudoun County Virginia's year-long, award-winning, Try Poetry 2010 initiative. The Kwame Alexander Papers, a collection of his professional and personal documents, is held at George Washington University's Gelman Library. Recently, Kwame served on the advisory board for Nikki Giovanni's The 100 Best African American Poems. He is currently the poet-laureate of LitWorld, a literacy organization dedicated to supporting the development of literacy in the world's most vulnerable communities. Visit him at **www.kwamealexander.com.**

Coming Soon: Wave: Twenty Love Poems (In English and Portuguese)

BRASIL

meu coracão crests
atop your raging waves where
even whales Samba

The type in this book was set in Franklin Gothic Medium for headings, and Palatino Linotype for text. Franklin Gothic is a realist sans-serif typeface designed by Morris Fuller Benton (1872-1948) in 1902. The typeface is one of over 200 typefaces designed by Benton. It is thought that this typeface was named after Benjamin Franklin. "Gothic" is an increasingly archaic term meaning sans-serif. At first only a Roman was released, but additional variants were added as Franklin Gothic became popular. Palatino Linotype is a version of the Palatino family that incorporates extended Latin, Greek, Cyrillic characters. It is one of the few fonts to incorporate an interrobang. Named after 16th century Italian master of calligraphy Giambattista Palatino (1515-1575), Palatino is based on the humanist fonts of the Italian Renaissance.

CPSIA information can be obtained
at www.ICGtesting.com
Printed in the USA
LVOW12s1425041017
551161LV00001B/70/P